by

*Remember
who you
are and
who loves
you...*

THE

Little Book

— OF —

CELTIC
WISDOM

In the same series

THE

Little Book

— OF —

CELTIC WISDOM

John and Caitlín Matthews

ELEMENT
Shaftesbury, Dorset ◆ Rockport, Massachusetts
Brisbane, Queensland

© *John and Caitlín Matthews 1993*

First published in Great Britain in 1993 by
ELEMENT BOOKS LIMITED
Shaftesbury, Dorset SP7 8BP

Published in the USA in 1993 by
ELEMENT BOOKS, INC.
PO Box 830, Rockport, MA 01966

Published in Australia in 1993 by
ELEMENT BOOKS LIMITED *for*
JACARANDA WILEY LIMITED
33 Park Road, Milton, Brisbane 4064

Reprinted 1994
Reprinted 1995

Cover illustration: Riders of the Sidht by John Duncan
Courtesy of the Dundee Museum and Art Gallery
Designed and produced by BRIDGEWATER BOOKS
Printed and bound in Hong Kong by Excel Graphic Arts

British Library Cataloguing in Publication data available

Library of Congress Cataloging in Publication Data
Matthews, John. 1948-
The little book of Celtic wisdom/John and Caitlín Matthews
Includes bibliographical references.
1. Celts–Religion–Quotations, maxims, etc.
2. Wisdom–Religious aspects–Quotations, maxims, etc.
I. Matthews, Caitlín, 1952– II. Title
BL900.M47 1993
299'.16–dc20   93–34175

ISBN 1-85230-435-9

CONTENTS

THE CELTIC TAPESTRY

In this little book, we have woven together some of the threads which pattern the Celtic loom of existence. This tapestry explores five dimensions, drawing upon some of the names which the ancient Celts gave to the worlds beyond earthly existence. *The Land of the Living* explores the nature of our communion with the land and with life. *The Land of Youth* explores the heroic adventures of life's quest. On *The Plain of Delight* we linger to overhear the whispering of lovers. On *The Plain of Silver* we reawaken the memory of our deep vision. In *The Land of Promise* we may still glimpse the patterns of eternal wisdom.

For the Celts, there was no separation between life and experience, between the world of humanity and that of the spirits and creatures, or between nature and the subtle process of creation. Love and war, vision and struggle were lived out within the encompassing of the elements.

The nature of Celtic writing is visionary and the language reflects this in its complex rhythms and brilliant imagery. The very names of the characters have an incantatory quality. The freshness and the depth of vision still casts its spell over us today.

The material selected here is drawn from ancient and modern Celtic sources, a list of which will be found at the back of the book. Unless otherwise indicated all new translations are by the authors.

JOHN & CAITLIN MATTHEWS
Oxford, 1993

Chapter One
THE LAND OF THE LIVING

TIR NA mBEO

he sun smiles over every land,
A parting for me from the brood of cares:
Hounds bark, stags tryst,
Ravens flourish, summer has come!

ANCIENT IRISH VERSE

The journey begins in the Land of the Living, at sunrise. It proceeds ever in a sunwise direction, following the sacred circuit of the year through time and space. It is marked by the invocation of the powers of the universe, to clothe the traveller with a garment of spiritual protection:

I arise today
Through the strength of heaven:
Light of sun,
Radiance of moon,
Splendour of fire,
Speed of lightning,
Swiftness of wind,
Depth of sea,
Stability of earth,
Firmness of rock.[1]

Interwoven with the ninefold elements of the universe, the supplicant becomes identified with these powers, even taking them to be his judge if, by chance of some grave imbalance, he should cease to be so identified:

I will keep faith until the sky falls upon me
and crushes me, until the earth opens and
swallows me, until the seas arise and
overwhelm me.[2]

o runs the awesome oath, appealing to the elements as the foundations of the universe, to be the enduring witnesses of human promises. The elements witness all ritual action: the many-coloured winds bring different gifts and opportunities; fire and water are used by midwives to sain new-born children and by healers to cleanse people and animals of sickness; the sun and moon cast pathways of light upon the circuits of life; hills, rocks and waters are everywhere reverenced as places of power and memory-givers of initiation, treasure and song. For this is the Land of the Living.

The seasons themselves are elemental songs chanted by the stars:

Wind comes from the spring star in the East,
Fire comes from the summer star in the South,
Water comes from the autumn star in the West,
Wisdom, silence and death come from the
winter star in the North.[3]

In the prayer of the Four Stars of Destiny, the stars are the fourfold cloaks worn upon the circuit of life,

REUL NEAR, *Star of the East, give us kindly birth;*
REUL DEAS, *Star of the South, give us great love;*
REUL NIAR, *Star of the West, give us quiet age;*
REUL TUATH, *Star of the North, give us death.*[4]

The changing seasons teach us of both life and death, forming the web of our understanding. We may become aware of,

Orchil, the dim goddess who is under the brown earth, in a vast cavern, where she weaves at two looms. With one hand she weaves life upward through the grass; with the other she weaves death downward through the mould; and the sound of the weaving is Eternity, and the name of it in the green world is Time. And, through all, Orchil weaves the weft of Eternal Beauty, that passeth not, though her soul is Change.[5]

The goddess of the earth has many names and titles. As Beara, she brings the winter and shapes the rocks themselves:

> *When she struck a magic hammer lightly on the ground, the soil became as hard as iron; when she struck it heavily on the ground a valley was formed.*[6]

We welcome seasonal change as a regulator of our mood, like Merlin who, wandering in the Caledonian Forest, afflicted by madness after a battle, rebels against the winter which too closely reflects his own bare soul:

> *O that here were no winter or white frost! That it were spring or summer, and that the cuckoo would come back singing, and the nightingale who softens sad hearts with her devoted song . . . and that in new foliage other birds should sing in harmonious measures, delighting me with their music, while a new earth should breathe forth odors from new flowers under the green grass.*[7]

The singing of birds heralds the prime season when our hearts can expand and rejoice with new vigour, as the mighty hero, Fionn Mac Cumhail heralds the opening of Summer's wide door:

May: fair-aspected
perfect season:
blackbirds sing
where the sun glows.

The hardy cuckoo calls
a welcome to noble
Summer:
ends the bitter storms
that strip the trees of the
wood.

Summer cuts the
streams;
swift horses seek water;
the heather grows tall;
fair foliage flourishes.

The hawthorn sprouts;
smooth flows the ocean -
Summer causing it to
sleep;
blossom covers the
world . . .

The true man sings
gladly in the bright day,
sings loudly of May -
fair-aspected season.[8]

But though our own world begins to forget the intricate and sustaining figures of life's dance through the seasons, times and elements of the earth, there is still,

> *that small untoward clan, which knows the divine call of the spirit through the brain, and the secret whisper of the soul in the heart, and for ever perceives the veil of mystery and the rainbows of hope upon our human horizons, which hears and sees, and yet turns wisely, meanwhile, to the life of the green earth, of which we are part, to the common kindred of living things with which we are at one.[9]*

he Land of the Living teaches its lesson in simple ways, reminding us that the conscious and remembering spirit of the universe survives in all created life forms. But the apparent fragility of the living web cloaks an immense strength which can still be gratefully acknowledged:

> *Three slender things that best support the world; the slender stream of milk from the cow's dug into the pail; the slender blade of green corn upon the ground; the slender thread over the hand of a skilled woman.*[10]

Chapter Two
THE LAND OF YOUTH

TIR NAN OG

ruth in our hearts.
Strength in our hands.
Consistency in our tongues.

THE MOTTO OF THE FIANNA

To be young in those times was to be a hero;
to be a hero was to prove oneself the best: born
by strange births, living by wondrous laws,
achieving marvellous feats. Thus there is the
hero of Arthur's warriors, Gwalchmai, whose
name means Hawk of May, who 'never came
home without the quest he had gone to seek.
He was the best of walkers and the best of
riders. He was Arthur's nephew, his sister's son,
and his first companion.'

And Cuchulainn, the greatest hero of Ireland,
born to his mother after the god Lugh flew
into her drink in the shape of a May-fly,
is unforgettable in his bright glory:

> *He who sits in that chariot,*
> *Is the warrior, able, powerful, well-worded,*
> *Polished, brilliant, very graceful . . .*
> *His name is Cuchulainn,*
> *Son of Lugh, son of Dechtire,*
> *His face is like a red brilliant sunburst.*
>
> *Fast-moving on the plain like mountain mist;*
> *With the speed of a hill-hind,*
> *With the speed of a hare on level ground.*
> *The fast step – the joyful step -*
> *Of the horses coming towards us -*
> *Like snow hewing the slopes.*[11]

ot that Cuchulainn always looked so
fair. When seized with battle madness
a terrible transformation took place:

> *Within his skin he put forth an unnatural*
> *effort of his body: his feet, his shins, and his*
> *knees shifted themselves and were behind*
> *him; his heels and calves and hams were dis-*
> *placed to the front of his leg-bones, in condi-*
> *tion such that their knotted muscles stood up*
> *in lumps large as the clenched fist of a fight-*
> *ing man. The frontal sinues of his head were*
> *dragged to the back of his neck, where they*
> *showed in lumps bigger than the head of a*
> *man-child aged one month. Then his face*

underwent an extraordinary transformation:
one eye became engulfed in his head so far
that 'tis a question whether a wild heron
could have got at it where it lay against his
occiput . . . the other eye on the contrary
protruded suddenly, and of itself so rested
upon his cheek. His mouth was twisted awry
till it met his ears. His lion's gnashings
caused flakes of fire, each one larger than the
fleece of a three year old wether, to stream
from his throat into his mouth and so out-
wards. The sounding blows of his heart that
panted within him were as the howl of a
ban-dog doing his office, or of a lion in the
act of charging a bear . . .[12]

his we remember – as we remember Culhwch in the glory of his youth, riding to his cousin Arthur's court:

The youth pricked forth on upon a steed
with head dappled grey, of four winters old,
firm of limb, with shell-formed hoofs, having
a bridle of linked gold on his head, and
upon him a saddle of costly gold. And in the
youth's hand were two spears of silver,
sharp, well-tempered, headed with steel,
three ells in length, of an edge to wound the
wind, and cause blood to flow, and swifter
than the fall of a dewdrop from the blade of
reed-grass upon the earth when the dew of
June is at the heaviest. A gold-hilted sword
was upon his thigh, the blade of which was
of gold, bearing a cross of inlaid gold of the
hue of the lightning of heaven: his war horn
was of ivory. Before him were two brindled

white breasted greyhounds, having strong collars of rubies about their necks, reaching from the shoulder to the ear. And the one that was on the left side bounded across to the right side, and the one of the right to the left, and like two sea-swallows sported around him. And his courser cast up four sods with his four hoofs, like four swallows in the air, about his head, now above, now below. About him was a four-cornered cloth of purple, and an apple of gold was at each corner, and every one of the apples was of the value of a hundred cattle. And there was precious gold of the value of three hundred cattle upon his shoes, and upon his stirrups, from his knee to the tip of his toe. And the blades of grass bent not beneath him, so light was his courser's tread as he journeyed towards the gate of Arthur's palace.[13]

All heroes were proclaimed at birth to be astonishing. Cuchulainn slew the great hound of Culainn the Smith and received his name, which means 'Hound of Culainn' as a result. While still a child he mastered the finest chariot horses in the King of Ireland's stable; his skills and his strength were both prodigies. Fionn, Ireland's other great champion, was always of a more meditative mien, though his abilities were nonetheless considerable. Placed in the charge of two women warriors (a Roman author wrote that the women of the Celts were even more ferocious and terrifying than their men) the youthful hero soon displayed his remarkable accuracy with the bow:

> On a certain day the boy went out alone,
> and saw ducks upon a lake. He sent a shot
> among them, which cut off the feathers and
> the wings of one, so that a trance fell upon
> her; and then he seized her and took her with
> him to the hunting booth. And that was
> Fionn's first chase.[14]

ater, when Fionn formed the band
of premier warriors known as the
Fianna, their training reflected their leader's
own abilities:

> *There was no man taken until he knew*
> *twelve books of poetry. And before any man*
> *was accepted, he would be put into a deep*
> *hole in the ground up to his middle, and he*
> *having his shield and hazel rod in his hand.*
> *And nine men would go the length of ten*
> *furrows from him and would cast their spears*
> *at him at the same time. And if he got a*
> *wound from one of them he was not thought*
> *fit to join with the Fianna. And after that his*
> *hair would be fastened up, and he put to run*
> *through the woods of Ireland, and the Fianna*

following after him to try could they wound him, and only the length of the branch between themselves and himself when they started. And if they came up with him and wounded him, he was not let join them; or if his spears trembled in his hand, or if a branch of a tree had undone the plaiting of his hair, or if he had cracked a dry stick under his foot, and he running. And they would not take him among them till he had made a leap over a stick the height of himself, and till he had stooped under one the height of his knee, and till he had taken a thorn out of his foot with his nail, and he running his fastest. But if he had done all these things, he was of Fionn's people.[15]

uch things were the norm among the bright ranks of the heroes. But they knew other ways as well, and were gentle by turns, and wise. Cormac, known as the Irish Solomon, gave a list of things that pertained both to king and warrior:

Be not too wise, nor too foolish,
be not too conceited, nor too diffident,
be not too haughty, nor too humble,
be not too talkative, nor too silent,
be not too hard, nor too feeble.
for:
If you be too wise, one will expect too much of you;
if you be foolish, you will be deceived;
if you be too conceited, you will be thought vexatious;
if you be too humble, you will be without honour;
if you be too talkative, you will not be heeded;
if you be too silent, you will not be regarded;
if you be too hard, you will be broken;
if you be too feeble, you will be crushed.

'It is through these habits', adds Cormac, 'that the young become old and kingly warriors'.[16]

➤ 26 ⬅

Just as their births and deeds were extraordinary, so were their deaths. None more than that of Cuchulainn, who took upon him the whole of the army of Maeve of Connacht; and might have won were it not for the treachery of the Morrigan, the battle goddess whose love he had refused. Then, terribly wounded, he went to a lake-side to drink,

and he went to the pillar stone that is in the plain, and he put his breast-girdle round it so that he might not die seated nor lying down. Then came the men around him, but they durst not go to him, for they thought he was alive . . .

Then came birds and settled on his shoulder.

'There were not wont to be birds about that pillar' said Erc, son of Cairpre. Then Lugaid arranged Cuchulainn's hair over his shoulder, and cut off his head . . .

But the soul of Cuchulainn appeared to the thrice fifty queens who had loved him, and they saw him floating in his spirit-chariot over Emain Macha . . . [17]

nd when they were gone to the Land of
Promise, others remembered the warriors:
the women for their beauty and the men for
their cruel skills, as in this lament for the great
hero-king Niall of the Nine Hostages, uttered
by a chorus of mourners:

Eyelashes black, delicate, equal in beauty,
and dark eyebrows:
The crown of the woad, a bright hyacinth:
That was the colour of his pupils.

The colour of his cheeks at all seasons,
even and symmetrical;
The fox-glove, the blood of a calf – a feast without
flaw!
The crown of the forest in May.

His white teeth, his red lips that never reproved in
anger
His shape like a fiery blaze
Overtopping the warriors of Erin.
Like the moon, like the sun, like a fiery beacon
Was the splendour of Niall:
Like a dragon-ship from the wave without a flaw
Was Niall, Echu's son.

Darling hero of the shining host!
Whose tribes are vast, a beloved band:
Every man was under protection when
We used to go to forgather with him.[18]

Chapter Three
THE PLAIN OF DELIGHT

MAG MELL

hree sparks that kindle love:
a face, demeanour, speech.

TRIADS OF IRELAND

Mag Mell, the Plain of Delight, is home to
many lovers: Trystan and Esyllt, Diarmuid and
Grainne, Culhwch and Olwen, names that still
evoke a shiver of delight, as we witness their
still living beauty and their often woeful fate.
Who could fail to love Olwen, 'White
Footprint', as she appears in the old Welsh tale
of Culhwch:

The maiden was clothed in a robe of flame-coloured silk, and about her neck was a collar of ruddy gold on which were precious emeralds and rubies. More yellow was her head than the flower of the broom, and her skin was whiter than the foam of the wave, and fairer were her hands and her fingers than the blossom of the wood anemone amidst the spray of the meadow fountain. The eye of the trained hawk, the glance of the trice-mewed falcon was not brighter than hers. Her breast was more snowy than the breast of the white swan, her cheek was redder than the reddest roses. Whoso beheld her was filled with her love. Four white trefoils sprang up wherever she trod.[19]

Culhwch fell in love with Olwen before ever he saw her; Peredur, a great hero, could become rooted by the very memory of his love, evoked by blood in the snow, and could turn aside from his quest because of it:

> *A shower of snow had fallen the night before, and a hawk had killed a wild fowl … And the noise of [Peredur's] horse scared the hawk away, and a raven alighted upon the bird. And Peredur stood, and compared the raven and the whiteness of the snow, and the redness of the blood, to the hair of the lady that best he loved, which was blacker than jet, and to her skin which was whiter than the snow, and to the two red spots upon her cheeks, which were redder than the blood upon the snow.*[20]

Such beauty may seem perilous, and sometimes could be so. When the enchanters, Math and Gwydion, in Welsh tradition, made a wife for their cousin Llew Llaw Gyffes, they took 'the blossoms of the oak, and the blossoms of the broom, and the blossoms of the meadow sweet, and produced from them a maiden, the fairest and most graceful that ever man saw . . . and they gave her the name of Blodeuwedd', which means 'Flower Face'.

Poor men, they should have known better, for a woman made of flowers has no notion of faithfulness, and when Blodeuwedd met the handsome huntsman Gronw Pebyr she fell in love with him:

> *And he gazed on her, and the same thought came unto her, so that he could not conceal from her that he loved her, but he declared unto her that he did so. Thereupon she was very joyful. And all their discourse that night was concerning the affection and love which they felt one for the other, and which in no longer space than one evening had arisen.*[21]

Like many another, their love was doomed; for when their plot to kill Llew was discovered, Gronw paid the price with his death, and Blodeuwedd was turned into an owl by her vengeful creators.

Love could be perilous in many ways. Once, three of the greatest of the Fianna, the warrior race of Ireland, visited a house in which lived a beautiful young girl. And after supper one by one they courted her. But she was Youth itself, and to each one of them she gave the answer: 'I belonged to you once, but I will never belong to you again'. But when it came the turn of Diarmuid O'Duibhne, so handsome was he that she said:

'Come over here to me, Diarmuid . . .
and I will put a love-spot on you, that no
woman will ever see without giving you
her love'. So Diarmuid went over to her,
and she put her hand on his forehead, and
she left the love-spot there, and no woman
that ever saw him after that was able to
refuse him her love.[22]

his by itself is a most fearful gift, for from that time Diarmuid must keep a hat pulled over his brows, lest every woman he sees fall in love with him. But when he meets the bride of his lord, the hero Fionn McCumhail, both are lost:

> It chanced . . . the cap fell from him, and
> Grainne was looking out at him as it fell,
> and great love for him came on her there and
> then. And she called her serving-maid to her,
> and bade her bring the great golden cup that
> held drink for nine times nine men from the
> sunny house. And when the serving-maid
> brought the cup, she filled it with wine that
> had enchantment in it . . . And all that
> drank of it fell into the same heavy sleep.
> And when they were all in their sleep,
> Grainne rose up softly from the seat where
> she was, and she turned her face to Diarmuid
> and she said: 'Will you take my love,
> Diarmuid son of Duibhne, and will you
> bring me away out of this house tonight? [23]

orced to flee, they lived the life of outlaws in the wild, their love preserving them through every trial and test. Their wandering gives the land a new story: the places where they lie are ever after known as the Beds of Grainne. Once, watching as Diarmuid sleeps, Grainne sings a song of loving sleep to her lover:

> *Sleep a little, a little little*
> *for there is nothing at all to fear.*
> *Diarmuid, son of Duibhne,*
> *sleep here soundly, soundly,*
> *Diarmuid, to whom I have given my love.*
>
> *It is I will keep watch for you,*
> *child of shapely Duibhne;*
> *sleep a little, a blessing upon you,*
> *beside the well of the strong field,*
> *my lamb from above the lake,*
> *from the banks of the strong stream . . .*

O heart of the valour of Western lands
my heart will go near to breaking
if I do not see you every day.
The parting of the two of us
will be the parting of two children
of the one house;
It will be the parting of life from the body,
Diarmuid, hero of the bright lake of Carmen.[24]

arted they were in the end, and Diarmuid
had his death at the hands of the jealous
Fionn. Jealousy, too, drove King March, whose
wife, Esyllt, fell in love with the handsome
stranger Trystan, to pursue them when they
fled, like Diarmuid and Grainne, into the Forest
of Celyddon. When they would not come out,
March complained to Arthur, who sent men to
demand of Trystan that he give up Esyllt.
Trystan would not, yet peace was made in the
end through a strange bargain:

Arthur conversed with the two of them in turn, and neither of them was willing to be without Esyllt. Then Arthur adjudged her to one while the leaves should be on the wood, and to the other during the time that the leaves should not be on the wood, the husband to have the choice. And the latter chose the time when the leaves should not be on the wood, because the night is longest during that season. And Arthur announced that to Esyllt, and she said: 'Blessed be the judgement and he who gave it!' And Esyllt sang this englynn [verse]:

Three trees are good in nature:
the holly, the ivy and the yew,
they keep their leaves throughout their lives:
I am Trystan's as long as he lives.[25]

L ove, doomed or fulfilled, is a bright thread in the weaving. Faery women, beautiful and perilous at once, beckon from the sides of the Hollow Hills. Aengus Og, god of love and youthfulness, kindles death and life in the hearts of his subjects:

> *There is an old legend that Aengus goes to and fro upon the world, a weaver of rainbows . . . He is a deathless comrade of the Spring, and we may well pray to him to let his green fire move in our veins; whether he be but the Eternal Youth of the world, or be also Love, whose soul is youth; or even though he be likewise Death himself, Death to whom Love was wedded long, long ago.[26]*

Chapter Four

THE PLAIN OF SILVER
MAG ARGATNAL

*hree candles that illume every darkness:
truth, nature, knowledge.*

TRIADS OF IRELAND

We come to the Plain of Silver, which is also
the place of vision, magic and enchantment.
It is the place we enter naturally at twilight,
when the worlds mesh and meld at the
between light:

> *I saw the Weaver of Dreams, an immortal
> shape of star-eyed Silence; and the Weaver of
> Death, a lovely Dusk with a heart of hidden
> flame; and each wove with the shuttles of
> beauty and Wonder and Mystery . . .
> Come unto me, O Lovely Dusk, thou that
> has the heart of hidden flame.*[27]

Without the enchantment to kindle the beckoning flame of mystery and wonder, we lose touch with the on-going story of the soul.

The Celtic poet is in tune with the universe, able to access any level of its connected life-forms and to draw back wandering souls into the nets of the story. The poet is a prophet, a kist of knowledge, the memory of the people, a shaman who draws upon the spirits of the universe. The golden chain of tradition passed into the hands of the gifted people as they incubated their sacred poetry in darkness, lying upon beds, with stones upon their chests to keep them wakeful, and turned their inner ears towards the Otherworld:

The house of memorizing for our gentle boys,
the trysting-place of youthful gathering,
shining embers red and bright,
that was the forge of memory . . .

Blessings upon their noble nature,
to whom complex poems were no hardship;
to that beloved gathering of poets,
the darkest verse was daylight dawning.[28]

All creativity begins in this sacred darkness of listening meditation for, upon the Plain of Silver, the onset of darkness heralds the telling of tales. We hearken to stories of kings, queens, younger sons and daughters, magical beasts, quests and dangers, monsters and faeries, and forget our own troubles, setting our soul beside that of the adventurer and seeking the ultimate quest.

Those who have no stories, sing no songs, are poor indeed. But however scanty our store of treasure, we can always access the door of dreams for soul's enrichment:

Had I the heaven's embroidered cloths,
Enwrought with golden and silver light,
The blue and the dim and the dark cloths
Of night and light and the half-light,
I would spread the cloths under your feet:
But I, being poor, have only my dreams;
I have spread my dreams under your feet;
Tread softly because you tread on my dreams.[29]

he soul's treasury is enriched and enlightened by whatever we experience upon our journey: for there are,

Three candles that illume every darkness:
truth, nature, knowledge.[30]

Dawn and twilight are the times for changing for there is no ending of life in this place. Living things may change their cloaks, yet they never pass out of existence. All that *is* remains, vulnerable to memory, rich with remembrance. Lives pass smoothly into other existences so the pattern of the weaving is unbroken.

There is no sense of creator as weaver, only the incantation of poetry and song which simultaneously creates what it utters. As Amergin Whiteknee, chief poet and shaman of the Milesian invaders, greets the land of Ireland from his ship, he remembers all existences of which he has partaken in flesh and in vision. He makes this rhapsodic song of self-introduction to the land, speaking of his creative powers by way of strange kennings: of the cattle of Tethra as the stars arising from the sea, greeting the ox of the moon:

I am a wind on the sea,
I am a wave of the ocean,
I am the roar of the sea,
I am an ox of seven exiles,
I am a hawk on a cliff,
I am a tear of the sun,
I am a turning in a maze,
I am a boar in valour,
I am a salmon in a pool,
I am a lake on a plain,

I am a dispensing power,
I am a spirit of skilful gift,
I am a grass-blade giving decay to the earth,
I am a creative god giving inspiration.

Who else clears the stones of the mountain?
Who is it who declaims the sun's arising?
Who is it who tells where the sun sets?
Who brings cattle from the house of Tethra?
Upon whom do the cattle of Tethra smile?
Who is this ox?
Who is the weaving god who mends the
thatch of wounds?
- The incantation of a spear,
- The incantation of the wind.[31]

n Amergin's mystical identification with all
things, he becomes one of the physicians of
the soul, reweaving the scattered elements of life
into a new wholeness. This is the task of Celtic
poets, whose skill is to bring the soul to the point
of vision, rest and stillness. The music of their
healing skill is known by three strains: the laugh

strain, which raises the spirits; the sorrow strain, which causes the release of tears; and the sleep strain, which brings rest to troubled souls.

Sometimes the pattern of the living web is interwoven with animal transmigrations, when the soul goes for healing into the body of a creature. There are many who endured from earliest times by this means, to have the companionship of other creatures than humans. This primal knowledge endowed the transmigrant with great power of memory. Tuan mac Carill is one such who has travelled a circuit of births in different shapes. The last survivor of his race, he continues in a series of animal shapes and is able to relate the history of Ireland to those who come afterwards. He experiences the vigour of each animal:

I was king of the boar-herds in Ireland, and I still went the round of my abode when I used to come into this land of Ulster at the time of my old age and wretchedness; for in the same place I changed into all these shapes. Therefore I always visited that place to await the renewal . . . I remembered every shape in which I had been before.[32]

s stag, boar, hawk and salmon he lived successively until he was caught and eaten by Carill's wife.

Again I remember the time that I was in her womb . . . I also remember when speech came to me, as it comes to any man, and I knew all that was being done in Ireland, and I was a seer.[33]

he subject of these transmigrations becomes a tradition-bearer to later ages, for he can descend the animal-ladder to the times before and emerge with ancient knowledge unguessed at by younger people who have remembrance only of their human lives. The animal forms in these transmigrations are related to the ages of the world and to the reordering and remembering of creation.

Creatures are the guardians of pre-human memory, which is one reason why shamans have innerworld, animal helpers. In our times, animals are important teachers, patiently enduring and revealing the truths which humankind ignores, reminding us that each life-form has its purpose in the universe, that certain memories of wisdom are in danger of being lost forever unless we reconnect with the enchantment which feeds our soul.

The Plain of Silver restores us to memory, as Merlin is restored to himself by the poet

Taliesin who therapeutically recreates the universe for his friend in bardic incantation. Merlin's soul returns to him and he cries:

> *Oh King, through whom the order of the*
> *starry heavens exists, through whom the sea*
> *and the land with its pleasing grass give forth*
> *and nourish their offspring and with their*
> *profuse fertility give frequent aid to*
> *mankind . . . I was carried away from myself*
> *and like a spirit I knew the acts of past*
> *peoples and predicted the future. Then since*
> *knew the secrets of things and the flight of*
> *birds and the wandering motions of the stars*
> *and the gliding of the fishes, all this vexed*
> *me and denied a natural rest to my human*
> *mind by a severe law. Now I have come*
> *to myself . . .*[34]

Many of us hopelessly contemplate,

> *The world without wonder, the world with-*
> *out mystery! That indeed is the rainbow*
> *without colours, the sunrise without living*
> *gold, the noon void of light . . .*[35]

How can the soul or the world be re-enchanted once it has lost its grasp of the golden links of tradition? Can we catch the old song which restores the enchantment? Celtic story speaks of seven questers who return from the perilous inner journey to bring cauldron or Grail back from the innerworlds.

> *And such joy did [they] bring about, that there-*
> *upon did the people repeople the land after the*
> *great destruction . . . and the waters which ran*
> *not, and the fountains which flowed not, for*
> *that they had been dried up, ran forth amidst*
> *the meadows. Then were the fields green and*
> *bountiful, and the woods clad in leaves the day*
> *that the Court of Joy was found.*[36]

The Court of Joy, wherein the restoring vessel abides, can still be discovered. The wisdom of the ancient earth's enchantment still resounds in the deep recesses of the human heart, leading us to memory and gladness.

Chapter Five
THE LAND OF PROMISE

TIR TAIRNGIRE

my chair is in Caer Siddi,
Where no-one is affected with age
or illness . . .
It is surrounded by three circles of fire.
To the borders of the city comes the
ocean's flood,
A fruitful fountain plays before it,
Whose liquor is sweeter than the finest wine.

TALIESIN, THE DEFENCE OF THE CHAIR

The Land of Promise is also called the Land of
Heart's Desire. The restlessness of divine
discontent usually presages the journey to this
land wherein we discover that such a desire is
only the fulfilment of our deepest nature:

The desire of the fairy women: dew.
The desire of the fairy host: wind.
The desire of the raven: blood.
The desire of the snipe: the wilderness.
The desire of the seamew: the lawns of the sea.
The desire of the poet: the soft low music of the
    Tribe of the Green Mantles.
The desire of man: the love of woman.
The desire of women: the little clan.
The desire of the soul: wisdom.[37]

This land has many shapes, just as it has many names and locations. Such names are themselves a litany of longing, giving rise to dreams and visions in which the Otherworld appears, beckoning, again and again.

*There was a large fortress in the middle of a
plain with a wall of bronze around it. In the
fortress was a house of white-silver, and it
was half thatched with the wings of white
birds. A fairy host of horsemen were at the
house, with lapfulls of the wings of white
birds in their bosoms to thatch the house . . .
Then Cormac . . . saw another royal strong-
hold, and another wall of bronze around it.
There were four palaces therein. He entered
the fortress and saw a vast palace with beams
of bronze, its wattling of silver, and its
thatch the wings of white birds. Then he saw
in the enclosure a shining fountain, with five
streams flowing out of it, and the host in
turn drinking its water . . . He entered the
palace. There was one couple inside awaiting
him. The warrior's figure was distinguished
owing to the beauty of its shape, the
comeliness of its form, and the wonder of
its countenance. The girl along with him,
mature, yellow-haired, with a golden*

head-dress, was the loveliest of the world's women. Cormac's feet were washed by invisible hands. There was bathing in a pool without the need of attendance. The heated stones themselves went into and came out of the water.[38]

Many travellers choose to make a voyage to the Blessed Realms of the West in a small boat, there to encounter many tests, challenges and changes. They often take these voyages or *immrama* seemingly by accident; they become exiled from their own land, and enter the realm of the wide and trackless ocean.

There is a distant isle,
Around which sea-horses glisten:
A fair course against the white-swelling surge -
Four pedestals uphold it.

A delight to the eyes, a glorious range
Is the plain on which the hosts hold games:
Coracle contends against chariot
In the silver-white plain to the southward.

Pedestals of white bronze underneath
Glittering through ages of beauty:
Fairest land throughout the world,
On which the many blossoms drop.

An ancient tree there is in bloom,
On which birds call to the hours:
In harmony of song they all are wont
To chant together every hour.

Colours of every shade glisten
throughout the gentle-voiced plains:
Joy is known, ranked around music,
In silver-cloud plain to the southward.

Unknown is wailing or treachery
In the homely well-tilled land:
There is nothing rough or harsh,
But sweet music striking on the ear.

Without grief, without gloom, without death,
Without any sickness or debility -
That is the sign of Evin:
Uncommon is the like of such a marvel . . .[39]

his Otherworld of wonders is a still living
dimension to which all mortals can relate.
It transcends but also intersects the reality we
call 'everyday life'. It is the source from which
inspiration comes. It is accessible through that
burning glass of the soul – the imagination –
which is nothing less than our doorway to
the Otherworld, through which come the
dreams, visions and ideas which transform
ordinary reality.

One day the young poet Nede fared forth till
he stood on the margin of the sea, for the
poets believed the brink of water to be the
place of poetic revelation. He heard a sound
in the wave, even a chant of wailing and
sadness, and he marvelled thereat.

    So the youth cast a spell upon the
wave, that it might reveal to him the cause
of its moaning.[40]

hese are the lands of wisdom itself, where
the dreamer travels nightly and the poet
accesses the power of his words. For when a
poet is asked whence he comes, what better
answer can he give than this?

I move along the columns of age,
Along the streams of inspiration . . .
Along the fair land of knowledge
The bright country of the sun;
Along the hidden land which by day the
moon inhabits;
Along the first beginnings of life . . .[41]

In the circle of being let this prayer for long life lead us along the streams of inspiration in the fair lands of knowledge, from the Land of Promise back to the Land of the Living:

I invoke the seven daughters of Ocean
who weave the threads of the sons of age.
Three deaths be taken from me,
three life-times be given me,
seven waves of surety be granted me.
No illusions disturb my journey,
in brilliant breastplate without hurt.
My honour shall not be bound by oblivion.
Welcome age! death shall not corrupt the old.

I invoke the Silver One, undying and deathless,
may my life be enduring as white-bronze!
May my double be killed!
May my rights be upheld!
May my strength be increased!
May my grave not be dug!
May death not visit me!

May my journey be fulfilled!
I shall not be devoured by the headless adder,
nor by the hard green tick, nor by the
headless beetle.
I shall not be injured by a bevy of women
nor a gang of armed men.
May the King of the Universe stretch time for me!

I invoke Senach of the seven aeons,
fostered by faery women on nurturing breasts.
May my seven candles never be extinguished!
I am an indestructible fortress,
I am an unassailable rock,
I am a precious jewel,
I am the prosperity of the weak.
May I live a hundred times a hundred years,
each century in turn.
The fullness of their brew my sufficiency!
The encircling of the Spirit's fortress be about! [42]

ur fivefold journey has led us through the looms of life, with courage, love, vision and inspiration as our guides. With these many-coloured skeins may we weave the pattern of our spiritual tapestry to give covering for lives yet unborn.

SOURCES

1. Kuno Meyer (trans.), *Selections from Ancient Irish Poetry*, Constable & Co., 1913. **2**. Caitlín Matthews, *The Celtic Book of the Dead*, Harper Collins, 1992. **3**. Fiona MacLeod, *Iona*, Heinemann, 1927. **4**. Ibid. **5**. Fiona MacLeod, *The Silence of Amor*, Heinemann, 1919. **6**. Donald A. MacKenzie, *Wonder Tales From Scottish Myth & Legend*, Blackie & Son Ltd., 1917. **7**. Geoffrey of Monmouth, *Vita Merlini*, trans. J. J. Parry, University of Illinois, 1925. **8**. John Matthews (trans.) in *From the Isle of Dreams*, Floris Books, 1993. **9**. Fiona MacLeod, *The Birds of Angus Og*, Heinemann, 1927. **10**. Kuno Meyer, op. cit. **11**. Adapted from the translation by Hector Maclean in *Lyra Celtica*, Patrick Geddes, 1896. **12**. E. Hull, *The Cuchullin Saga*, David Nutt, 1898. **13**. Lady Charlotte Guest (trans.), *The Mabinogion*, J. M. Dent, 1937. **14**. T. P. Cross and C. H. Slover (eds.), *Ancient Irish Tales*, Henry Holt, 1936. **15**. Lady Augusta Gregory, *Gods and Fighting Men*, John Murray, 1904. **16**. Kuno Meyer, op. cit. **17**. E. Hull, op. cit. **18**. Adapted by the authors from the translation by Kuno Meyer in *Selections from Ancient Irish Poetry*. **19**. Lady Charlotte Guest, op. cit. **20**. Ibid. **21**. Ibid. **22**. Lady Augusta Gregory, op. cit. **23**. Ibid. **24**. Adapted by the authors from the translation by Lady Gregory in *Gods and Fighting Men*. **25**. T. P. Cross, (trans. 1912). Reprinted in *A Celtic Reader*, John Matthews, Aquarian Press, 1991. **26**. Fiona MacLeod, *The Birds of Angus Og*, Heinemann, 1927. **27**. Fiona MacLeod, *The Silence of Amor*, Heinemann, 1919. **28**. Caitlín Matthews (trans.), *Aonar Dhamhsa Eidir Dhaoinibh*, anonymous bardic poem of 18th-century Ireland. **29**. W. B. Yeats, *The Wind Among the Reeds*, 1899. **30**. Kuno Meyer, op. cit. **31**. Caitlín Matthews (trans.). **32**. Kuno Meyer (trans.), *Scél Túan maic Cairill* in *Voyage of Bran*, David Nutt, 1895. **33**. Ibid. **34**. Geoffrey of Monmouth, op. cit. **35**. Fiona MacLeod, *The Birds of Angus Og*, op. cit. **36**. Sebastian Evans, in *Quest of the Holy Grail*, J. M. Dent, 1898. **37**. Fiona MacLeod, *Naoi Miannain*, in *From the Hills of Dream*, Heinemann, 1929. **38**. T. P. Cross and C. H. Slover (eds.), 'Cormac' Adventures in the Land of Promise' in *Ancient Irish Tales*, Holt, 1936. **39**. Kuno Meyer (trans.), 'The Isles of the Happy', op. cit. **40**. Eleanor Hull, *The Poem-Book of the Gael*, Chatto & Windus, 1912. **41**. Ibid. **42**. Caitlín Matthews (trans.)